EVERYDAY KNOWLEDGE ABOUT YOUR

FINANCES

YOU DO NOT KNOW

JEROME T. SCOTT
LUTCF, LOMA, CPIA

Chosen Pen Publ

Fayetteville, NC

The Chosen Pen
1430 Hoke Loop Road,
Fayetteville, NC 28314.

ISBN: 978-1-952315-98-5
Jerome T. Scott
1. Non-Fiction
2. Business - Finance

To order additional copies of the resource, contact Chosen Pen Customer Service:
1420 Hoke Loop Road
Fayetteville, NC 28314
FAX orders to 910-868-3300
Phone orders to 910-818-6652
Website: www.chosepen.com
Printed in the United States of America.

TABLE OF CONTENTS

FOREWORD

Beginning this journey with Jerome, I always believed he was an individual with knowledge in whatever area he was involved in. We have known each other for close to 60 years and this has not changed as the years have passed.

I have spoken with him on different occasions about writing a book based on his knowledge of finances. I have seen him assist many individuals through the years and always believed a book would allow him to help even more people.

Jerome is known as “The Insurance Guy” in our area. He initially began in the insurance field as an administrator for a large insurance firm called Equitable Life Assurance in New York City, New

York. This was his introduction to this field, where he learned many principles that he has used to help so many. He worked for other companies as he continued along his professional path.

Today, Jerome is an insurance broker. This position allows him to meet his client's various needs with coverage that explicitly addresses their financial situation. His clients describe him as an honorable man who is a legend in the community. Jerome is known for his honesty and unfailing pursuit of fulfilling his clients' financial needs.

As you begin or continue your financial journey, please take time to absorb the habits Jerome recommends in this book. These habits will help you plan, build, and establish a solid financial future.

Here's hoping you will move forward with a clear vision for your future,

Gwen

Principles always have natural consequences. The more we know of the correct principles, the greater our personal freedom to act wisely.

STEPHEN COVEY

INTRODUCTION
DEDICATED TO YOU

I am here to guide you along the path of your financial plan. The financial arena is large and vast. There are many individuals who claim that they can assist you. I am not saying they are unable to be of assistance. I am saying that I know that my knowledge and experience is second to none.

I have a strong background in the insurance industry, with experience in risk management and financial planning. I have an MBA and continue furthering my industry knowledge through continuing education courses and certifications.

You've chosen to read this book because you're ready to take control of your financial future. I want to assure you that this is not just a book to read, but a tool to empower you. The information I'm sharing is only as useful as the commitment you make to put it into practice.

The reasons that individuals do not ask for assistance are not clear. Possibly, they do not know who to ask for assistance. They may not want to admit that they are having financial challenges. They may feel ashamed of their present financial state.

There are individuals who are desperate for a change in their situation, and with the right information, their situation could change. Many individuals could use financial advice, but they do not seek it. You are actively seeking financial advice right now since you are reading this book. Take the knowledge you gain by reading this book, put the information into action, take steps to change your situation, and change your current financial state.

Imagine the available options you will have for yourself and your family once you understand how to manage your finances appropriately. Get ready to take a life-changing journey where you learn how to control your finances and your future.

If you don't know where you
are going, you'll end up
someplace else.

YOGI BERRA

CHAPTER 1
SAVING FOR YOU

The question I will pose to you right now is: where are you going? The answer to this question relates directly to your finances. It is easy to observe in our society how different classes of people are affected by the amount of money they have at their disposal. Some individuals cannot think beyond today because they are unaware of how saving money can affect their future.

Creating a Savings Plan

I want you to consider the following questions thoughtfully and honestly. Part of your financial journey is identifying where you are today and achieving your goals.

- How are you saving your money for your future?
- How are you preparing your family for their financial future?

Saving money now is the first step in securing your financial future. How you plan and interact with money will directly affect your family's financial future. You have to decide how you would like to live in the future. Be honest with yourself and determine if you want to maintain your present standard of living or if you want to live even better than you are living now.

Many aspire to improve their financial state but are unsure how to reach their desired destination. Despite the aspiration, some are unwilling to take the steps necessary to improve their current situation. Since you are reading this book, I am sure you have decided to aspire and take action to create a better financial outlook for yourself and your family. The steps you take today are necessary to create the desired positive outcome.

Let's do some preliminary calculations. I'll give you space to write down your results.

1. Assume the amount it takes monthly to maintain your present status. Write it on the line below.

   ____

2. What is the amount of your current yearly income? Write it on the line below.

   ____

3. To maintain your present state of living, you should save a minimum of 10% of your current income. Due to economic fluctuations, you can decide to save 15%.
   A. Decide what percentage you want to save, 10% or 15%. ___________
   B. Calculate the amount to save by multiplying the percentage you selected (0.10 or 0.15) by the answer for #2

above. Write that number here.

____

4. The amount in 3B is how much you would need to save per year. Divide the answer by 12 to reveal your monthly savings goal.

____

Your current age and the age at which you want to retire are not included in these calculations but are worth considering. Since most people look towards retirement at 65, I recommend increasing your savings to 25%.

You can utilize the same calculation above to determine the amount of your income to save, replacing 0.15 with 0.25.

Retiring well is the best reward for a lifetime of hard work. Our society has changed since I started my career. In the past, I was motivated to move up within the company I worked for. I was rewarded with different items and recognition that generations today would not ever receive since changing jobs is part of the work environment now. Very few individuals remain at the same place of employment for longer than two years. Plus, many companies no longer offer incentives for employees to be employed with them for a prolonged period. This, however, should not stop you from planning for your future.

Savings options are not based on your place of employment, and financial health is not based on your profession or career. Your financial future and financial health are directly related to your plan to save and how you optimize these savings.

Successful retirement is based on careful planning. When you choose to retire, the amount of money you receive from Social Security benefits and monthly pension will probably not equal the amount of your last paycheck before you retire. That is why saving is so essential for your future.

Other Considerations

Can you now see how important saving money is for your future? It is the first step in having a healthy financial future.

Here are some additional questions to consider as you plan your financial future. Take some time to consider these questions and write down your answers so you can formulate your ideal future. Planning helps you consider all your options and allows you to determine what you do not want.

Documenting your thoughts will also help you visualize where you are headed and motivate you to initiate your savings. This document will also allow you to discuss things with your family and other individuals you care about.

- What type of living conditions are you in search of at your retirement time?
- Do you have a current hobby you want to expand on when you retire, such as golfing?
- Would you like to live in a community that focuses directly on this hobby, (a golfing

community, a beachside community, a community in the mountains)?

- Would you desire to have room and space for extended family or grandchildren?
- Are you in search of an area close to medical facilities?
- Do you have a certain location you are interested in living in?
- What is the cost of living in the location you are interested in living in?
- Do you want to travel?
- What other factors may be vital for you at the time of retirement?

Tax Considerations

As you formulate your retirement vision, it is essential to consider taxable areas. Taxable areas are parts of your income, property, or purchases that the government can tax. These can include the money you earn from a job, investments, property you own, things you buy, and even money or property passed down after someone dies.

If you are unsure of what areas you should investigate directly, I will list some important things to consider here.

Investigate the following:

- **Taxation of earned and investment income** - taxes paid on the money made from working (earned income) and things like stocks, bonds, or savings (investment income).

• **Pension income taxation** - tax paid on money received from a retirement plan.

• **Taxes on Social Security benefits –** a tax that may have to be paid on Social Security benefits received if the income is above a certain amount.

• **State property tax** - tax paid each year to the state based on the property's value, such as a house or land.

• **State sales tax rates** - the tax percentage added to the price of items bought in stores. (This rate varies by state.)

• **Estate taxes** – a tax that may be taken from the value of a person’s property or money after they die, before it is passed on to their heirs

Be sure to consult your accountant for a full explanation of these terms and how they may or may not apply to your financial planning needs.

Let's look at a practical example. Take 2% of a salary of $25,000 per year with compounding interest. 2% of this amount would be calculated to be $59,800 after saving for 30 years. The percentage saved in each paycheck would be $20. I recommend saving a higher percentage. This example shows that saving anything is beneficial even if you don't start saving 10% to 15%. The key is that you start and remain consistent in saving. Just start today.

When it comes to creating a saving plan, age does not matter. You are never too young to start saving for your financial future, even if you don't have all the answers. You will need money to live on as you continue to age, there is no question about that. If you are older, it is never too late. You just need to start.

Where to Save

Where should your money go? In a cookie jar? Under your mattress? In a piggy bank? These are places that people have used in the past and are still using today. As age-old as these locations are, so are the available options provided by financial institutions and agencies.

Sometimes, people are apprehensive about saving money with a commercially available option. However, this is a result of little knowledge and information on the subject. As you are saving your money, you should consider what type of financial savings vehicle is right for you. What you choose is based on what is available to you, what money you have to start with, and your risk preference. By becoming more educated in ways to save your money, you can take control of your financial future and feel more capable of managing your wealth. You may also seek the assistance of a financial advisor to help you make the best decision.

Financial vehicles to consider:

- Savings account

- Money market account
- Certificate of deposit
- Mutual fund
- Annuity
- Stocks

A Case Study

In thinking about saving, on more occasions than you'd care to admit, you've probably decided that now is not a good time to start. You've factored in the cost of living for your household, things such as the rising price of food vs the lack of increase in our paychecks, or the amount you currently bring in is just enough to clear everything. The flip side to that coin is that if you truly believed those things, you wouldn't be reading this book. Let's take a look at a case study from a former client who felt the exact same way.

Meet Ann, a young woman in upper 20's making ~$40,000 year as an administrative assistant. As a single parent, she thought there was no way she'd be able to save for her financial future.

During the time I worked with her, writing checks was a popular payment method. I instructed her to write a check for everything that she purchased. In writing checks, it was good practice to keep track of them with the checking ledger or register. Using the register was a good way for her to see exactly where her money was going as well as how much she was spending. The use of check registers was to keep a running balance of the available funds in your account, instead of just guessing or making a semi-informed estimate.

It did not matter how big or small the purchase was, she was instructed to write a check to pay for whatever she bought. When she listed the amount of the purchase, she was to make it for $1.00 more than the amount she actually paid. For example, if the purchase was for $25.00, I instructed her to add one dollar to the amount, so that purchase would be $26.00 in her ledger. She started this practice at the beginning of the month and at the end of the month we met to balance her checkbook and reconcile her ledger with her bank statement.

In that month, she wrote 30 checks. This resulted in an additional $30.00 that she could use for savings. This simple, yet effective practice, showed her that she was able to save money and not have it affect what she needed to do financially during the month. The success of the as a first month encouraged her to save more and she was able to begin saving $50.00 to $55.00 per month as she continued with the practice I recommended.

Two of her financial goals were to save money for her children's future and secure a life insurance policy. Her savings habit allowed her to reach both goals when she initially believed neither were options for her.

Your Turn!

You probably do not write as many checks as this young lady if you even use checks for anything right now. However, you make purchases with cash or a debit card. When you make these purchases, I challenge you to put aside $1.00 for your savings immediately. For every purchase you make during a month, put a dollar aside. You may think that this is not going to be a lot. In the first month, you will be surprised at how much you have saved using this easy and practical principle.

Another strategy for increasing your monthly savings is to have 10% of your paycheck deposited into a savings or money market account every time you are paid.

Start doing this today: Save 10% to 15% of your income for the future.

A penny saved is a penny earned.

BEN FRANKLIN

CHAPTER 2
TOOLS FOR YOU

Budgeting is essential for you to identify where your money is going, as well as to plan where it should be going. A budget as a document that captures how much money you have coming into your possession and then where your money is going as you use it.

Your budget should include allotments for things such as rent/mortgage, phone, gas expenditure, utilities, car, food, education, pet, insurance, and any additional expense that is a recurring cost for you.

I am often asked what type of budget sheet an individual should use. My answer is the budget sheet you are most comfortable with. There are many ways that you can create your sheet. The most important part of a budget sheet is that you can use it consistently. A budget should be created to assist you in reaching your financial goals.

Budgeting allows you to determine where and how much money you want to spend. It then provides a real-time illustration of how much money you spend during a given time. Your budget serves as a guide for your spending and saving. It is a fluid document that can change as your life circumstances change.

You will be thankful that you started a budget and even more glad when you see that you are able to operate within the guidelines of your budget. You should review your budget at the end of the month to see how well you utilized your guide. Problem areas will become more evident the more you use your budget and as you remain consistent. Remember, reviewing and adjusting as needed is key.

Using a budget is a practice in which you need to be truthful with yourself, as well as with your spouse and family. Involve them in the budgeting process so they are ware of what spending parameters are present in your household as well as what you are working towards in the financial area.

Please do not attempt to go around your budget or omit certain spending from it. Also do not attempt to go beyond what you have budgeted for a certain area knowingly. Keep your financial goals at the forefront of your mind and let your goals provide the reinforcements you need to remain consistent in following your budget.

I am aware that when many people hear the word budget, they tense up and believe it will hinder what they can do and restrict what they are able to do. People believe it is a method of control that they do not want to subject themselves to. Being on a budget can lead to financial creativity.

When you observe individuals that you define as 'wealthy', please understand that they have taken steps to maintain this wealth and instill in their children the ways to maintain wealth. One of the main ways of doing this is utilizing a budget, consistently. Individuals who are wealthy utilize a budget and use practices where they are able to have the comforts of life, but they are not wasteful with their money. They also do not make attempts to impress others. They focus on themselves, their own family members, and their personal financial goals.

In order to reach your saving goals, you have to actually save money. A budget will aid you in your savings journey. As you are establishing your budget, remember to get organized by:

- Setting financial goals
- Determining your present situation

- Controlling spending
- Limiting credit card debt.

Maintaining Focus

Ten simple ways to stretch your money and maintain the focus on your budget:

1. Create a spending plan that includes what you want your financial future to include.
2. Pay yourself while you also save money.
3. Track your spending, even for those small optional purchases.
4. Live within your means. Before you purchase something, ask yourself, "Do I really need this?"
5. Shop for value.
6. Minimize debt.

7. Eat many meals at home, as dining out can be expensive and is often unnecessary.
8. Reduce housing costs as much as possible.
9. Reduce transportation costs.
10. Create an emergency fund to use when financial emergencies arise.

The list above can assist you with staying focused on your financial goals and maintaining your savings plan. A budget is one of the essential components of a healthy financial journey. The items included on this list are easy to complete; however, you have to remain consistent in your actions to see the benefits. As you begin following your budget, you can see your situation changing in real-time.

Using a budget creates actionable steps that you can use daily to allow yourself the ability to move towards what you desire your financial future to create for you. Start with one or two goals. As you begin to reach these goals, add more additional goals. Most people attempt to accomplish all of their goals at one time. This can create a sense of feeling overwhelmed which can result in inaction.

To address your financial goals and budget, you must be an active participant. Sometimes, people want all their goals to happen at once, or they want their goals to be accomplished quickly with little effort on their part. This is a steady process that requires consistent actions to achieve success. Reaching goals on your financial journey will not happen immediately or all at once.

Be encouraged and remain consistent.

Your Action Step: Create your budget today!

20 years from now you will be more disappointed by the things you didn’t do than the ones you did do.

MARK TWAIN

CHAPTER 3
PLANS FOR YOU

Let us do some dreaming. This is where you can be creative and enjoy yourself. Imagine how you want your future to look in 5, 10, or 15 years. Now, let's think about how your life will be when you reach the average retirement age of 65 or the age you would like to retire. Maybe you want to retire at 65 years old or maybe you want to continue to work.

As you are dreaming?! What does your future look like? Get into as much detail as possible.

Where do you want to live? How do you want to live? Do you want to downsize or increase space? Have you considered living in a retirement community? These are just a few questions that can shape how you should save now for your future goals and the type of financial vehicles you will utilize for saving. Before we move forward, take some time to write down your answers to the questions.

The challenge many individuals face as they age is that they have not planned far enough in advance. To many, the future does not consist of anything further than the next month or year. When planning your financial journey, you have to think more long-term. People are aging in better health today than at any other time before. They are also living longer, sometimes in excellent health and sometimes with challenging health conditions. If you are closer to the beginning of your life journey, you may not have even considered long term care insurance.

Individuals often believe that they will need less money as they get older. Look back at your budget from chapter 3. Your total living expenses will only shrink slightly as you age. Surprisingly, your living expenses usually only decrease by 20%. That means whatever your budget is now, you will need 80% of that amount as you mature. Were you aware of this fact? This is something else you need to keep in mind as you travel on your financial journey. You may require more finances than 80% of your current living expenses, depending on the needs of your family members like your parents, children, grandchildren or siblings, if you choose to assist them at times.

Currently, you are accumulating money through employment or other streams of income you have. When you retire or reduce your work activities, you will not be accumulating money like you are now. How long will the money you have been saving now last when you are spending it in the future without actively replenishing it?

Ask yourself these questions as you plan for your future and write your answers down:

- What is your credit score today?
- Would you be able to receive a loan if you applied for one?

- How much money do you expect to receive on a regular basis when you retire?
- What sources do you expect to receive money from when you retire?
- How much money do you have in savings?
- Do you have enough life insurance to protect your dependents? The amount of life insurance should be calculated based on your annual salary and should be three to five times this amount.
- What is your net worth?
- Do you have the appropriate investments for the current state of the economy?

Were you able to answer most of the questions? If yes, even with estimates, you are already way ahead of most individuals. People can get so busy making a living that they do not check into their financial health. Giving attention to your financial health is essential. Taking charge of your finances gives you the ability to do what you want in life. You have to create a plan for your future and a plan for your finances.

As you live out your plan, you will accomplish financial objectives and make progress. Consider this important fact moving forward, as you continue to live in the future you have planned, the process of creating and addressing financial objectives will also continue. Self-reflection and making goal updates and/or changes will be necessary. Unforeseen circumstances and situations can arise unexpectedly as well.

To formulate your plan, you can take the following action steps:

1. Gather information. The information needed will vary from individual to individual. However, a great start is to make sure you have a list of your assets and liabilities and know your net worth. Information about income and expenditures is also necessary. Take note of your investments, insurance policies, employee benefits, wills, trusts, and inheritances.
2. Establish your objectives with a timeline. Do not skimp this step, as having clear, measurable objectives strengthens the foundation for your steps.
3. Analyze the gathered information.

4. Formulate your goals.

Another Case Study

I interacted with a gentleman in retirement who was able to follow a financial plan earlier in life. He was ready to live the way he wanted to since he did not have to go to work each day. He was retired and ready to live based on the plan he had made.

When I followed up with him, he informed me he was actually very stressed from his current living situation. His house had new establishments built all around. This was not how he had envisioned his future when he was retired. He did not feel comfortable where he lived. He wanted to move even though he had previously made different plans. He felt like he had no other choice but to relocate. He made a financial plan in the past and followed it to save for his future. His past actions provided him with the ability to have options. He was successful in saving for his financial future. Because of this, he could relocate to a place where he felt more comfortable and enjoyed himself more.

Think about your plan for the future. Plan well so you can pivot to a different plan if necessary. Individuals usually want to be comfortable as they mature. Having adequate finances allows you to do this for yourself with ease. Planning is the key to aiding you in creating your financial future.

Take the time: Plan your future

Greatness is not a functional circumstance. Greatness, it turns out, is largely a matter of conscious choice and discipline.

JIM COLLINS, GOOD TO GREAT

CHAPTER 4
DISCIPLINE FOR YOU

This next part of your financial journey is going to have you perform even more serious self-reflection. You will have to look internally and evaluate your ability in the area of discipline. Discipline focuses on how well you can set personal boundaries and remain true to them to allow you to progress to your goals. Everything we have discussed so far hinges on this very characteristic - How disciplined are you in the various areas of your life? Are you a focused individual when you have a goal in front of you? You have to realize that everything with your financial future is based on how well you can discipline yourself.

One thing that can aid you in staying true to your discipline is seeking someone else to support you in your journey. You need to establish an accountability partner, someone in your life with whom you can discuss your goals. This same person needs to remind you of your goals when it appears that you are moving off track from where you should be. In this relationship, there needs to be a sense of trust and honesty from both individuals.

In a marriage, your accountability partner can be your spouse. You both should be working towards a future together that includes good financial health. One way to do this is to look at your relationship to define a few things. Determine who is a saver and who is a spender. Do you both exhibit the same characteristics? In my experience, two savers can make a marriage prosper. One saver and one spender can make marriage work as well. There are just more involved conversations over finances. Having a relationship with two spenders usually doesn't last. Why, you ask? Because there will be no money left for either person to spend, creating unhappiness. Someone will leave the relationship in search of more resources.

Looking at your current relationship and spending characteristics may help you identify why you are experiencing some of the challenges you already have. Money can be the cause of many problems in a relationship. Many times, trying to solve these problems without the proper knowledge can make these issues unsolvable. Beginning your financial journey or strengthening it using this book can aid in helping you solve some of those financial questions.

I also say if you desire to be in a relationship, you should seek out a saver to become involved with, especially if you are a spender.

If you are not married, find a family member, a close friend, or even a financial advisor who you can share your personal information with. Having an accountability partner is imperative for your discipline.

If you are unable to initiate the discipline needed in the area of your finances, the outcome will be devastating for you and your family. Financial issues can have long range implications on many parts of your life.

I hear you asking, "What should I do if my discipline is not that strong?" My answer to you is simple. You must have an accountability partner who will make sure you follow your plan. Your partner must be comfortable asking you questions about your financial decisions, and you must feel comfortable answering them. Hopefully, this partner has a plan and budget of their own as they can serve as a financial role model for you.

Here are other ways to strengthen your discipline:

- Write down your financial goals and keep them where you are able to review them each day
- Make small incremental steps that allow you to work towards a larger goal
- Reward yourself when you reach a goal
- Seek out other individuals who have reached goals you are interested in achieving
- Ask questions when unsure what to do next; speak with professionals.

Take the steps: Strengthen your discipline.

Change will not come if we wait for some other person or some other time. We are the ones that we've been waiting for. We are the change that we seek.

BARACK OBAMA

CHAPTER 5
REWARDS FOR YOU

So far, looking at your financial habits may have been a bit challenging, as this is not something that you regularly focus on. It may be a new skill and area of learning for you. I encourage you to stay on track to meet your financial goals and encourage you to continue to learn and investigate ways that you can focus on your financial journey. There are numerous ways to dig deeper into this area and become even more proficient. Continue along with the process that you have decided to initiate. Make the changes. Take the steps.

As you move along in your journey, reward yourself at regular intervals. Avoid using a "what's in my pocket" form of spending to provide yourself with rewards. You need to know how much you will allow yourself to spend on yourself. Create a line item in your budget that will allow you to reward yourself while continuing to maintain your budget.

Give yourself an allowance for incidental spending. Operating within spending boundaries will allow you to feel rewarded while still allowing you to maintain your path to your goals. These boundaries will also help prevent overspending.

When formulating your goals, think about how excited you will be when you can reflect on where you started and where you are. Along the way, you need to congratulate yourself. This does not mean that as you reach micro-goals or short-term goals, you ignore the budget you have established or change your savings patterns. It is the complete opposite. You include in your budget the exact date and reward you will receive once you reach a particular milestone. For larger accomplishments, you can create larger rewards for yourself.

Some rewards can be small. You can also plan for larger rewards that take time to work up to. Take time and save up funds to go on a dream vacation that is all paid for versus going on vacation and creating more bills you are responsible for when you return. Travel with a greater peace of mind as you have already taken care of everything before traveling. If traveling is not something that you desire, you can come up with another large reward that you enjoy, like a shopping excursion or a concert. Your reward needs to be something that brings you joy.

In the beginning of your financial journey, rewarding yourself may seem challenging as what you desire may be out of your present budget. However, as you stick to your goals, rewards can develop into something greater.

Initially, rewards can require some creativity on your part. You have to be able to identify activities you enjoy that require a limited amount of money and reward yourself with those things first.

Here are some examples of low-cost rewards:

- Take a nap
- Create a private space in your home where you go and relax
- Get an ice cream treat you enjoy
- Get a coffee that you enjoy
- Watch a favorite show
- Go to a museum
- Read a book

All these activities should be used as a reward and not something that you experience regularly.

You work hard: Reward yourself!

My formula for success is
rise early, work late and
strike oil.

JP GETTY

CHAPTER 6
SUCCESS FOR YOU

As you begin to put these concepts into practice in your life and take actions toward making improvements for yourself and your family, you should see changes in your financial outlook. Based on my years of experience, I chose to speak to certain aspects of your financial portfolio that individuals who are early in the financial field may not focus on.

Sometimes it is easier for people to relate to individuals who physically work out, because those are changes that are visible to the eye. Financial may be visible, but they are more difficult for others to see and congratulate you on. Let me be the first to encourage you to keep it up! Practice your financial fitness just like you would practice weightlifting. You have to give yourself time to develop your financial muscles. Don't stop too soon! Be aware that it will take time!

I have given you some key concepts throughout this book that you can immediately put into practice today. I will also leave you with a few more keys to strengthening yourself financially. I am giving you these keys because I know if you use them, you will see changes that will forever affect you. You can also share these concepts with other individuals you care about by purchasing a copy of this book for them, meeting with your family and explaining the importance of financial health, scheduling an appointment with a financial advisor.

Here are some key activities for you to focus on:

- Set short- and long-term financial goals
- Evaluate your progress towards your goals and adjust as appropriate
- Increase your savings with the goal of saving at least 10% of your income
- Contribute to an IRA or another plan that you can use
- Pay down credit card balances
- Pay off credit card balances monthly to avoid finance charges

- Review your insurance and legal documents regularly

There are numerous layers to financial health. Continue to develop yourself in this area. The information you are learning is helping you take the necessary steps to an even healthier financial future. Yes, this book contained a lot of information. I am knowledgeable in this area.

Remember: don't compare yourself to anyone else. Comparing yourself to someone else may make you feel like you have a long way to go, which can prevent you from starting the process of making changes in your situation.

Take the first step today by choosing one of the concepts and immediately making it part of your daily routine.

Let's review the key concepts from this book:

- Savings - maintain a portion of your income as savings for your future
- Budgeting - create a document letting you know where you will spend your money and how much will be spent as well as saved
- Planning - create a pathway to follow on your financial journey so you know where and why you are headed in a specific direction
- Discipline - maintain focus on your financial journey by maintaining discipline to reach your goals
- Rewards - allow yourself something that you enjoy after you reach a goal to keep yourself encouraged along your journey

This information may seem unattainable. There are so many pieces that need to be put together, but that doesn't mean you cannot perform all the necessary steps. Take your first step today.

Welcome to your financial journey!

COMMITMENT FOR A SUCCESSFUL FINANCIAL JOURNEY

I ______________________________ (print your name) agree to make the following commitments for a successful financial journey:

I. Mental Commitment by using the concepts in this book

II. Objective Commitment by:

  a. Being effective and efficient.
  b. Presenting ownership of all family properties.
  c. Planning for transfer of asset inventory by gift, trust, and will.
  d. Having Adequate and available money to meet known and anticipated future needs.

e. Creating effective plans for the ongoing management of family asset inventory beyond disability or death

III. Advisors Commitment

a. To choose advisor(s) for legal, accounting, trust, insurance, and investment matters.

b. To adhere to the direction and coordination of the advisors.

IV. Quality Commitment to be involved in the process.

V. Review Commitments for period updating and an annual review.

____

SIGNATURE

____

DATE

Made in the USA
Monee, IL
04 November 2026

67376110R00046